THE
Archive Photographs
SERIES

WARTIME EXETER
AND
EAST DEVON

D Coy, 8th Devons, Territorial Army at Meavy Lodge, Yelverton,1939. Back row, left to right: -?-, S. Brain, B. Long, Dick Parkman (Axminster), -?-, -?-, Sam Davis (Axminster), D. Kneebone (Dawlish), Jim Grinter (Axminster), Cyril Davis (Axminster), C. Hoard, Jim Searle (Colyford). Second row: Pte Buckingham (Axminster), Jim Watts (Seaton), -?-, -?-, -?-, -?-, Jack Bastone (Beer), -?-, George Voysey (Musbury), Tom Packham (Axminster), Bill Hine (Axminster), Cecil Sansom (Axminster), -?-, Pte Dawson (Axminster). Third row: Pat Butler (Colyton), Bob Pike (Honiton), Pte Vinnicombe, Cyril Chick (Axminster), Tommy Gooding (Colyton), Wilf Tratt (Axminster), -?-, Peter Lakeman (Seaton), Sam Voysey (Musbury), Jim Bastone (Seaton), -?-, Bert Mason, -?-, -?-. Fourth row: Sam Davey (Axminster), -?-, Pte Brenchley, Jack White (Axminster), Jack Spiller (Musbury), Lt Pugsley, -?-, Capt Batten, Rodney Denner (Exmouth), CSM Harry Channon (Budleigh Salterton), CQM S. Harvey (Exmouth), Ern Sloman (Axminster), -?-, John Fry (Axminster). Fifth row: George Morgan (Axmouth), Peter Harris (Seaton), Bert Loud (Seaton), -?-, -?-, Wilf Goodhall (Axminster), Pte McCriel, Clifford Powell (Axminster), Jack Parker (Axminster), Bert Hussey (Axminster), Syd Real (Colyton), George Potter (Colyton). Front: -?-, Pte Gooding (Budleigh Salterton), Sammy Ayres (Axmouth), Cpl Pollard, Vic Muggeridge (Colyford).

THE
Archive Photographs
SERIES

WARTIME EXETER
AND
EAST DEVON

Compiled by
Les Berry and Gerald Gosling

CHALFORD

First published 1996
Copyright © Les Berry and Gerald Gosling, 1996

The Chalford Publishing Company
St Mary's Mill, Chalford,
Stroud, Gloucestershire, GL6 8NX

ISBN 0 7524 0324 9

Typesetting and origination by
The Chalford Publishing Company
Printed in Great Britain by
Redwood Books, Trowbridge

Contents

Seaton Red Cross was formed in 1916 when the late Maud Holmes (front row, second from the left), a member of the Axminster detachment, was asked to form a detachment in Seaton for staffing at Ryall's Court. The matron and two sisters were appointed and, with the help of Seaton members who had been enrolled and trained, the hospital was soon ready for the arrival of the first wounded soldiers. Between the two wars membership fluctuated but Devon 110, as it was known, continued to work in the district. It was to give outstanding service to the town during the Second World War and continues to do so to this day. It is said that wounded soldiers claimed VAD stood for 'very adaptable dames'!

The Devonshire Regiment memorial in the Regiment's chapel at Exeter Cathedral.

Introduction

Yes, makin' mock o' uniforms that guard you while you sleep
Is cheaper than them uniforms, an' they're starvation cheap:
An' huslin' drunken soldiers when they're going large a bit
Is five times better business than paradin' in full kit.
Then it's Tommy this, an' Tommy that, an' 'Tom 'ow's yer soul?'
But it's 'Thin red line of 'eroes' when the drums begin to roll –
The drums begin to roll, my boys, the drums begin to roll,
O it's 'Thin red line of 'eroes' when the drums begin to roll.

In an age when nationalism is said to be dead, when children no longer learn the real truth about a glorious past, when anything and anyone goes as long as they do not extol the glories of the British race, it is, perhaps, fitting to return to England's first poet, Rudyard Kipling. He knew the glories of the past, he lived in an age when many of its pages were still being written, and he knew that the country's defenders had been scorned when not needed.

It is different today; two world wars have seen to that. And if hundreds of old men who wait patiently in the cold, and often damp, November air to march past the Cenotaph simply to pay their respects to the comrades who never came home cannot convince the scoffing trendies, surely the outpourings of a nation's heart on 8 May 1995 must. That is the real Britain, the Britain that stood firm for four years just outside Ypres, marched steadfastly forward on the Somme, laughed on the way home from Dunkirk, put out their 'Business as Usual' signs outside flattened shops in the East End, marched from El Alamein to Vienna with the Eighth Army, the longest advance in history, pounded hell out of the Reich's industrial centres, brought guns and grain across the Atlantic to a beleaguered homeland, the Britain that was in both world wars from Reveille to Lights Out and did not need to be bombed into either.

This book tells us of some of Exeter and East Devon's part in that past. From dim and remote days on the rim of the Empire on which the sun was said never to set (because God could not trust the English in the dark!), down to the Gulf War. Evocative pictures will remind those of us who lived through often heady days what it was like. A younger generation cannot fail to be surprised that so many pictures show happy faces. We are, after all, according to England's second poet, William Shakespeare, a 'Happy Breed'.

And I am happy to recommend this book to the reader. Les Berry and Gerald Gosling have given us an admirable cross section of life in wartime Exeter and East Devon and it is fitting that they end with a picture of the Royal British Legion, whose ceaseless efforts have done so much to make Kipling's poem redundant. They are all a 'thin red line of 'eroes' today, even when the drums have fallen quiet.

Frank Huddy, Chard, 1996

One
Land of Hope and Glory

Exeter & South Devon Volunteer Rife Corps at their first inspection in the Castle Yard, Exeter, 6 October 1852.

In 1794 George III sent out a proclamation asking for people to mobilize and take up arms against Napoleon's expected invasion. The proclamation required each town and village to bring about its own militia and be responsible for its own defence. One Company formed in this way was the Axminster Volunteers, and they were accepted into the East Devon Legion on 6 June 1794. Their declaration to the Crown said 'We the Volunteers (of Axminster) enrol ourselves as a Company for the protection and security of the Town and Neighbourhood of Axminster and the adjacent county not exceeding six miles, and under the sanction of an Act of Parliament lately passed, entitled an Act for encouraging and disciplining Volunteer Companies.' They served without pay, unless they served outside their own district or were requisitioned by the Lord Lieutenant of the County or in case of an actual invasion. They also provided their own uniforms. Left is a private of the Axminster Volunteers (1794-1802), and below is a private of the Axminster Company of the East Devon Legion (1803-08).

William 'Soldier' Mitchell of
Axminster proudly wears his Indian
Mutiny medals. William, always
known as 'Soldier', first served with
the 9th Lancers at the age of 19, and
then the 7th Hussars. He served in
India for twenty-four years, fighting
throughout the infamous Indian
Mutiny. His medals have bars for
Lucknow, Delhi 1857-1858,
Chilianwala and Goojevat. He was
discharged on a pension on 11 July
1865 and died at Axminster aged 78
on 4 December 1900. His Army
number was 732.

The 1st Exeter & Devon Volunteers
line up for parade in Bedford Circus,
c. 1879.

Officers and NCOs of C Company 1st Volunteer Battalion of the Devonshire Regiment at Exeter in 1888.

East Devon men are among the First Rifle Volunteers seen here in 1900 prior to departure for service in South Africa and the Boer War. Back row, left to right: Ptes C. Sidwell, J.G. Morrish, W. Hawkins, A. Agnew, W.G. Freeman. Second row: Ptes J. Tullidge, J.C. Tett, A.E. Tucker, A. Hoskins, H.J. Towning, L/Cpl W. Bazley, Pte C. Partridge, L/Cpl C. Hine, Ptes F.T. Weeks, T. Wilson. Third row: Ptes C.F. Gale, W.H. Cumes, F. James, Sgt R.G. Fugler, Cpl Sgt Cooper, Cpl F. Smale, Ptes P.E. Rattenbury, C.J. Stocker, H. Cornish. Front row: Ptes J.H. Wills, F.W. Tucker, Bugler E.A. Taylor, Ptes H. Hoskins, W. Palmer, G.W. Frost.

In 1910 two Territorial soldiers were drowned in the River Axe and were buried with full military honours at Axminster. The funeral procession leaves the Square, led by the firing party with rifles reversed.

In the churchyard the firing party fires the last salute. Note the iron railings that surrounded the entire church yard at the time. They went during a salvage drive in World War Two.

The 19th Devonshire Militia Band, 1900.

Boys of Exeter School Officers Training Unit in camp at Camelford in 1905.

The Boer War (1899-1900) was fought between the British Empire and the Dutch Boer republics of the Orange Free State and the Transvaal. The world at large, especially Germany, condemned the British and supported the Boers, largely forgetting that it was the Boers, under their president Paul Kruger, who declared war on Britain. The war is generally said to have been about the refusal of Kruger to enfranchise the Uitlanders (mainly British), and not about the Witwatersrand goldfields, as evidenced by the third verse of this jingoistic card printed in Axminster in 1900, 'We care not for their lands or diamonds, we care not for their gold'. But, with due regard to the acquisitive nature of the British Empire at the time, one might regard this with well-founded suspicion today.

Revd R. Turner (Colyton vicar and Volunteers padre) says goodbye at a special service with the Volunteers on the occasion of his departure from the living in Colyton.

REV. R. TURNER'S FAREWELL SERVICE TO THE COLYTON VOLUNTEERS

H Company (Axminster) 4th Battalion Devonshire Regiment Shooting Team in 1913, a highly successful year, with the Walrond Bowl, London Devonians' Cup, Birmingham Devonians' Cup, Manning-Kidd Cup, Milne Home Bowl and Escot Cup on show. Back row, left to right: Pte W. Russell, Pte G. Powley, L/Cpl J. Channing, Pte W. Gapper, L/Cpl F. Tuck, L/Cpl J. Coles, Pte J.N. Webster, L/Cpl G. Perham, Cpl F. Cawley, Pte W. Jeffery. Middle row: Colour-Sgt H. Clarke, Capt. W.G. Forward, Capt Percy-Hardman I.O.M., Colour-Sgt Instructor H.E. Roberts. Front row: Sgt S.O. Gill, Sgt A. Maeer, Sgt W. Perham.

The A Company 3rd Volunteer Battalion Devonshire Regiment (Axminster) shooting team for the annual 'Liverpool Devonians' Challenge Cup in 1903. The cup is on the right. The left-hand trophy was the ABID Trophy.

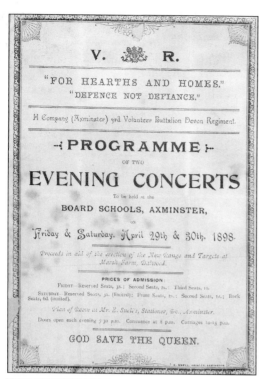

The outbreak of World War One, the 'Great War' to our fathers, ended a century of European peace for Great Britain. Apart from the Crimean War and 'other people's' European arguments, Britain's long Victorian afternoon and its Edwardian after-glow, typified by concerts of the sort illustrated left, was peaceful apart from alarms and excursions in the far-flung Empire. All that ended on 4 August 1914, evidenced by the grave faces as postman Harry Banks delivers the telegrams that announced the outbreak of World War One to Sidbury. Here, at Deepway, are, left to right: Mr Close of Bucton, Harry Banks, Jim Records, Hilda and Mrs Wilmington.

Two

The War
to end all Wars

The service section of the 2/4th Devons en route to the Persian Gulf in August 1915.

Tom Stamp bids farewell to his wife May and son Bill at their Dovecot, Cotleigh, home before going off for service with the Devonshire Regiment in World War One. Tom served through the war, coming back to Devon in 1919 after serving through many of the household-name battles, including Arras in 1917.

Tom Stamp (left, behind the man without a steel helmet) waits in the trenches with comrades in the Devonshire Regiment for the signal to go 'Over the Top' at Arras. Next but one to his left is Frank Reynolds from Newton Poppleford, who was severely wounded the following morning.

Women workers prepare to 'pick spuds' outside Exeter during World War One. Below they are engaged in the time-honoured West Country agricultural pursuit of 'dung-hauling'. It is interesting to note that all the ladies are wearing hats, which suggests the Victorian notion that sunburn was unfashionable was still in vogue.

Section Two, Exeter War Hospital, Christmas 1917.

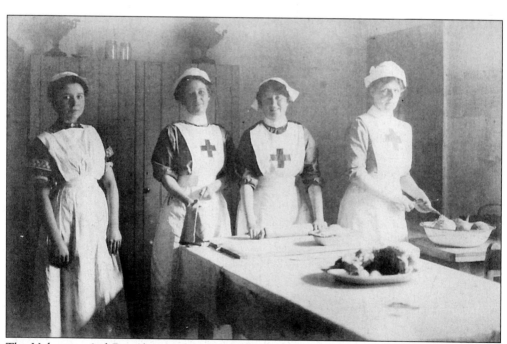

The Voluntary Aid Detachment (VAD) played an important part in caring for the wounded during World War One. Under their medical officer, Dr Steele-Perkins, they ran a hospital in High Street, Honiton, opposite St Paul's church.

Convalescent soldiers out for a drive in Honiton during World War One.

Men of the 41st Field Ambulance, RAMC, on Exmouth sea front in 1914. The Imperial Hotel is in the background.

Francis James Larcombe of Chardstock enlisted in the Somerset Light Infantry in 1915 at the age of 17. He was soon in France where he was wounded in the leg. After pouring copious draughts of iodine on the wound, he dug the bullet out with his own jackknife. When the Germans used gas on the Western Front for the first time he was among the early victims, and was so badly affected he was given six months to live. Devonians are nothing if not tough, however, and Francis lived until the age of 82 in 1980.

The Devons resting 'somewhere in France' during World War One. Of more than passing interest are the carriers behind plainly marked 'Devons'. In World War Two, when officialdom preferred to obliterate all traces of place names, such advertising would have been forbidden. In 1940, paranoid officialdom never ever realised that in the unlikely event of the the invading Germans not knowing where they were, they only needed to go into the post office and look at the name on the date stamps.

Suffragettism and 'Women's Lib' received much impetus during World War One thanks to the fairer sex's invasion of many of the jobs previously considered a male province. Here two munitions workers pose at Willey's Vulcan Works on Haven Banks, Exeter. Miss Florence Edwards is on the left.

The Devons take a meal break in Honiton in World War One. A little-known piece of military history is connected with the AA's attempts to pioneer the use of the 'horseless carriage' for military transport in Great Britain. They offered to transport a regiment by car from London to the coast and, despite some official disapproval, their offer was accepted. Because the officers had to tie their hats on with their handkerchiefs to prevent them blowing off, the army's chin strap was born.

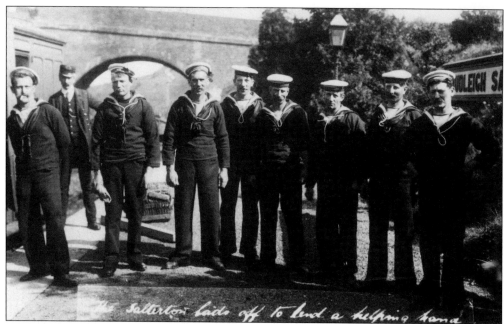

'The Salterton lads off to lend a helping hand.' This shows naval reservists about to leave Budleigh Salterton station in August 1914 to join the Fleet. There is a marked difference between the attention they receive and that given local soldiers called to the colours (below). They have a huge crowd and Budleigh's band to see them on their way.

Recruits waiting for the train at Ottery St Mary station on 1 September 1914. Much of the town have come out to see the men off, the ladies seizing the opportunity to parade in their Sunday best.

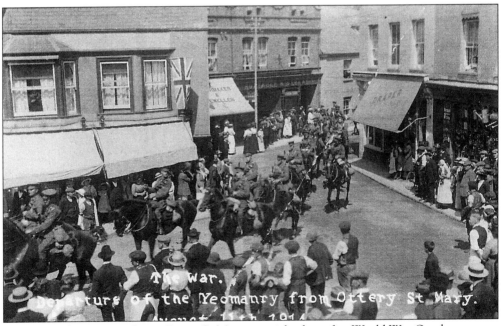

The (Devon) Yeomanry leave Ottery St Mary just eight days after World War One began.

Corporal Albert Farrant of Chardstock (right) with comrades of the Somerset Light Infantry in 1914 shortly after joining up. They were guarding Chard Junction against invasion; how paranoid officialdom can become in time of war!

Axminster members of the 1/4 Battalion, Devonshire Regiment, wait at Axminster station on 28 September 1914 for the train taking them to Perham Down, Salisbury Plain, en route for Southampton, from where they sailed for India on 9 October.

1/4 Devonshire Regiment in camp at Bulford Camp, Wiltshire, in 1914. Many Ottery St Mary men, including Cyril Godfrey, who sent this card to his mother at Victoria Place, are among the recruits seen here.

The First and Fourths later served overseas, including in Messopotamia (Iraq) against the Turks.

An elderly volunteer war-worker from Okehampton unloads sphagnum moss collected from an Exeter stream at a first-aid depot in the city during World War One. It was of special value for wound dressings.

A particularly plentiful source for the moss was at Pixies' Parlour, Head Weir, at Ottery St Mary, from where the local Boy Scouts would bag it and take it to Sidmouth Junction to meet the Red Cross trains.

World War One allotment cultivators at Exeter augmenting food supplies. One suspects the priest in the middle is only there for window dressing.

Mayoress's Depot for Gifts for Prisoners of War, 1918. This picture is taken outside St Pancras's church with Lady Owen in the centre. She ran the Mayoress's Depot for the comfort of fighting men.

Thought to be one of the first mobile first aid vans in Exeter (its No. 3 listing suggests at least two others), this van and, of course, its crew, rendered yeoman service during World War One.

Devonshire Regiment Territorials in camp around 1911 include Park Perriam from Budleigh Salterton (hatless in back row). 'No regiment has a more glorious record' Marshal Foch said of the Devons in World War One after the 2nd Battalion had been awarded the Croix de Guerre for its part in the Action at Blois de Buttes on 27 May 1918. To the thirteen Battle Honours on the Regimental Colour in 1914, another ten were added during that war. The Regiment served with distinction during the withdrawal of the BEF in May-June 1940, shared in the defence of Malta, served at Gibraltar and in India, and went back to France on D-Day.

Canadian soldiers passing through Honiton in World War One.

East Devon members of the 3/4 Battalion (A Company) Devonshire Regiment at Hursley Park Camp in August 1916. Back row, left to right: W.J. Rowland (Sidmouth), W. Bazley (Dalwood), ? Snelling (Ottery St Mary). Front: A.H. Collier (Beer), F. Bowden (Honiton), C. Newton (Seaton). Pte Bazley from Dalwood obviously had little faith in army issue braces; he is wearing a belt as well! It is not known how many of these men survived World War One, but Cyril Newton from Seaton certainly did. He went on to reach the grand old age of 97.

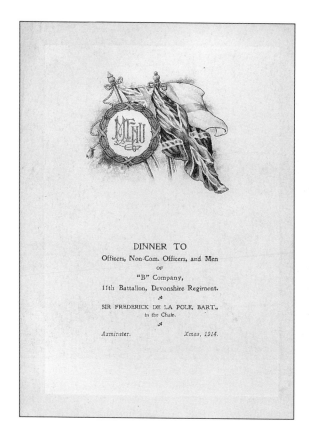

DINNER TO

Officers, Non-Com. Officers, and Men

OF

"B" Company,

11th Battalion, Devonshire Regiment.

SIR FREDERICK DE LA POLE, BART.,
In the Chair.

Axminster.   *Xmas, 1914.*

The menu card for a Christmas dinner for the Officers, NCOs and men of B Company, 11th Battalion, Devonshire Regiment at Axminster in 1914. Among local dignitaries present were Sir Frederick de la Pole Bt, the Revd E. Adams and Dr Langran. Note that the menu included good old English roast beef. Other delicacies on offer were pheasant, local vegetables, beer and cider (Devonshire, of course). All the liquid refreshment was provided by 'several gentlemen of the Town'.

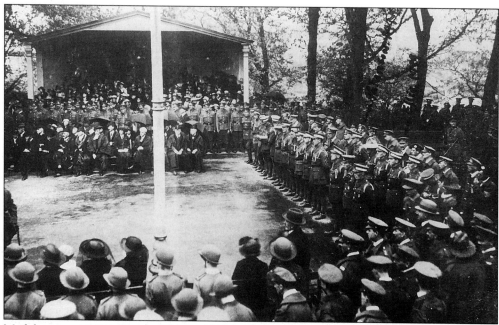

Medal presentation at Exeter, 18 May 1918.

Members of Exeter Cycling Club who took part as Territorials in Army Manoeuvres in 1912. Fifty-seven members served in the Great War. Those at home helped in many ways, including service in the Volunteers, the VAD and the Special Constables. Military Sports at the County Ground and concerts were arranged on behalf of the Mayoress of Exeter's Funds for the Soldiers. The club also entertained wounded soldiers every year at the County Ground (below).

Children who helped raise money, collect comforts and generally aid the war efforts during World War One received a certificate in recognition of their efforts. They were presented annually in different designs. Among Axminster children who received them were Evelyn Parker, above, in 1915, and William Manley, below, in 1916. They later married.

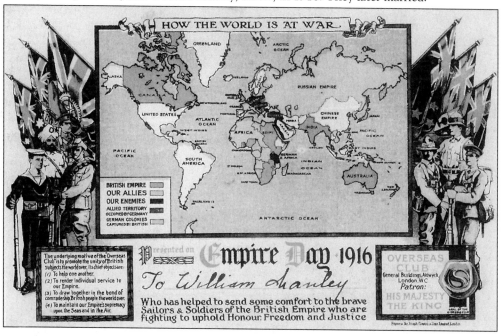

Army Pay Corps Sports, Exeter, 21 July 1917.

The First World War did not end on 11 November 1918, but a year later when the peace treaty was signed. This allowed time to manufacture various mementos, including commemorative mugs. In 1945, of course, there was no such warning. Here Honiton's mayor, Mr Seaborne Hook, prepares to distribute mugs to the children of the town in 1919.

Seaton's War Memorial at St Gregory's church after its first Armistice Day Service in 1921.

The plinth of Honiton's War Memorial bearing the names of the town's World War One dead is unloaded prior to its assembly outside St Paul's church in 1921.

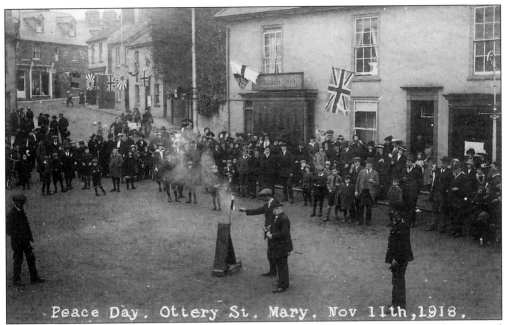

Peace Day. Ottery St. Mary. Nov 11th,1918.

Peace (Armistice) Day in Ottery St Mary on 11 November 1918 was marked with universal rejoicing. The picture above shows maroons being fired in the Square at 11 o'clock. Judging by the small crowd, the news was still circulating.

Peace Thanksgiving, Ottery St. Mary.

A year later in 1919 large crowds flocked to the same spot to give thanks for the actual signing of the Peace Treaty. A point of interest in the top picture are the Japanese flags in the background.

The Prince of Wales (later Edward VIII) unveils the County of Devon War Memorial on St Mary's Green in the Cathedral Yard at Exeter on 16 May 1921 (Whit Monday). Three copies of the names of the 11,601 Devon men and women who fell in the Great War were made on parchment bound in white vellum and embossed in gold. One, enclosed in an inscribed copper casket, was placed in a receptacle beneath the cross which is made of Dartmoor granite.

Ottery St Mary's war memorial in the parish church.

TO THE GLORY OF GOD AND IN UNDYING MEMORY OF THOSE FROM THIS PARISH WHO MADE THE GREAT SACRIFICE TO SAVE THE LAND THEY LOVED, 1914-1919.

Pte.	A.BAKER	Pte.	J.T.CUMMINGS	Pioneer	A.C.LUXTON	Pte.	W.SANDFORD
Pte.	J.BAKER	Cpl.	F.H.FIELD	Gnr.	G.H.LUXTON	Pte.	F.SHEPPERD
Cpl.	W.J.BARRETT	Lieut.Col.	P.C.GABBETT	Pte.	G.MAPKER	Cpl.	A.H.SHORT
Tpr.	A.BASTIN	Pte.	H.GODFREY	Sgt.	J.MARTIN	A.B.	F.G.SHORT
Pte.	C.D.BASTIN	Rfn.	C.W.HAKE	Pte.	F.J.MATTHEWS	Tpr.	W.H.SHORT
C-Sgt.	C.BATSTONE	A.B.	E.HAM		J.NELLWISH	Pte.	A.SLEE
Flt-Lieut.	S.L.BENNETT	Pte.	J.HAM	Pte.	A.MANLEY	Pte.	W.E.SLUGGETT
Pte.	A.G.BERRY	Pte.	D.J.HARDING	S-Sgt.	W.H.NORTH	Sgt.	J.SMITH
Pte.	F.W.H.BERRY	Pte.	A.HARRIS	Pte.	W.J.PALFREY	Pte.	F.TAYLOR
Pte.	F.BESS	Pte.	J.HARRIS	Pte.	T.H.PATCH	Pte.	W.THOMPSON
Pte.	W.BWARD		HILL	Pte.	J.FREEMAN	Cpl.	A.TOTTERDELL
Pte.	W.H.EDWARD	Pte.	E.F.HOOPER	Pte.	J.PIXEY	Pte.	W.TOTTERDELL
Pte.	A.BOVETT	Pte.	H.J.HOOPER	Pte.	W.PITTEGER	Pte.	F.TREMLETT
Pte.	O.BUTT	L-Cpl.	N.HOWARD	Pte.	T.PRATT	Pte.	F.VINEY
Pte.	A.F.BUTTERS	Sapper	F.G.HOWE	Pte.	H.PREG	Pte.	L.S.WELSMAN
Pte.	J.W.CANN	Staff	S.G.HOWE			A.B.	W.WHITE
Pte.	W.J.CANN	Pte.	W.HOWE	Pte.	F.RICHARDS	Sgt.	S.G.WHITE M.M.
Pte.	H.J.CHURCHMAN	Pte.	W.JAMES		J.RYDER	Pte.	A.WILSINGTON
Pte.	N.CHURCHMAN	Pte.	F.LANGDON		H.SALTER	Spear	E.WOODLEY
	J.F.OLEDFORD	Pte.	H.LEE	Pte.	H.SALTER	Pte.	W.F.WOODLEY
	J.CONNETT	Pte.	H.J.LIATT	C.S.M.	J.SMITH GUM	Gnr.	F.T.STILING
A.B.	M.CROSS	Blacksmith	J.LITTLEY	Pte.	S.K.SLTER		

The dedication of Sidmouth's war memorial at the Three Cornered Plot (now the Triangle) in 1920. It was later moved to the church.

A crowded Axminster churchyard for the dedication of the town's war memorial around 1921. In a later war the handsome railings which surrounded the church, part of which is seen here, went during salvage drives.

The dedication of Kilmington War Memorial in around 1921. Addressing the gathering is the Revd John Way, Kilmington's Baptist minister, who is supported by the Revd Charles Bull, Kilmington's vicar (1917-27). The Boy Scouts and Girl Guides are in attendance, and in the right background is the Axminster Town Silver Band.

Three

Half Time

Avro Anson aircraft at Exeter Airport shortly before the outbreak of World War Two.

Axminster Old Comrades' Association Dinner in the Drill Hall around 1920.

H Company (Axminster) 4th Battalion Devonshire Regiment Band in Axminster Square during that town's Peace Celebrations in 1919. Back row, left to right: ? Perham, Tom Young. Standing: Fred Enticott, John Channing, Charlie Larcombe, George Wench, Jack Chick, Freddie Coote, Jack Spiller, Walt Jeffries, Tom Mitchell. Sitting: Joe Clist, Sam Wench, Fred Wench (bandmaster), William Davey, Sam Bass.

4th Devons TA at Bulford Camp, Salisbury Plain, in 1934. Sgt George Moulding (Axminster) inspects the guard that won the 'best turned-out guard' trophy. They are, left to right: Cpl Joe Frampton, Pte Les Mitchell, Pte C. Davis (all from Axminster), and Pte Bradford (Honiton). Pte Bradford also won the individual award for best turn-out.

BULFORD FIELDS
Salisbury Plain

T. L. FULLER.
AMESBURY.

Although Lord Haldane (Secretary for War 1905-12 and responsible for many far-reaching and important army reforms) said that the Officers' Training Corps (OTCs) in the country were a waste of money (he reckoned they cost the taxpayer £45 a year per member), he might, if politicians ever admitted they were wrong, agree that they did provide a more-than-useful core of trained officers when World War One burst out on a largely unsuspecting Europe. Here the Allhallows School OTU can be seen drilling on the school playing field in Honiton. The pictures are dated 14 July 1914, halfway between the assassination of Archduke Franz Ferdinand at Sarajevo on 28 June, the 'Spark That Set The World Alight', and Austria-Hungary's declaration of war on Serbia which set World War One in motion. At that time Great Britain was largely unsuspecting of the Armageddon to come.

The advancing German armies had a shock when they first encountered the British Expeditionary Forces near Mons in 1914. So fast and accurate was their fire with the Lee-Enfield 303 rifles, that the Germans thought they were using machine guns. In what was still very much an agricultural economy at the time, shooting was second nature to countrymen of all classes, and the skill was honed to perfection in the militia and on rifle ranges such as this one at Ham Farm, Dalwood, in the 1920s, as well as, dare we add, through poaching. This range was built towards the end of 1899 for use by H Company (Axminster) 3rd Volunteer Battalion Devon Regiment, much of the money needed being raised locally by such events as the Evening Concerts billed right and held at the Board Schools in April 1898.

EQUAL RIGHTS AND FREEDOM.

O GOD of armies! guard our soldiers
   In this great hour of need,
And render kopjes, boulders, useless;
   Send Thou our guns God-speed.

WITHOUT Thine aid "Earth's mighty armies"
   Are scatter'd as the dust,
All men's devices, tactics, efforts,
   Wear out as metals rust.

WE care not for their lands or diamonds,
   We care not for their gold,
But care for "Equal Rights and Freedom"
   For all in Thine own mould.

ASSUAGE the wrath of envious nations,
   Guide them to see we've right,
And Britain's Empire firm and steadfast,
   Establish in Thy might.

WE ask again Thine aid, ALL-POTENT!
   To crush th' insidious foe,
That Justice, Christian Love, and Freedom,
   Henceforth may ever flow.
                  W.H.B.C.

AXMINSTER, JAN. 6th, 1900.

Exeter Royal Artillery Band, *c.* 1920, at St James Park football ground.

Allhallows School, Honiton Officers Training Corp being inspected by General Dew-Wyatt on the playing Fields in 1935. A thirteen-year-old Terry Glanville (later Dr Glanville) is second from the right. Horace Lee, the Officer Commanding, is extreme left. General Dew-Wyatt was to become a prisoner-of-war in World War Two.

Pte Les Mitchell of Axminster, aged 17, soon after joining the local (4th Devon) TA, at Honiton ranges where he won the Battalion Recruits Cup for rifle shooting in 1929.

Chardstock man Tony Brownsell joined the Somerset Light Infantry in December 1933 because of lack of local employment prospects, and served in India until the outbreak of World War Two, when he joined the Parachute Regiment. He took part in Operation Market Garden, the Rhine Bridges assault, and was captured at Arnheim. He was liberated in 1945 by the Russian army and returned to England for demobilization in December 1945 after twelve years with the colours. He is seen below fourth from left in the front rank on the King's (George VI) Birthday Parade at Poona in 1937.

The *Express & Echo* tells its readers that World War Two has begun.

Members of 163/55 LAA Regt at the TA Centre in Barrack Road, Exeter, in 1939.

Four
WW2 – Dad's Army

Topsham Platoon, Home Guard, parade in Budleigh Salterton around 1943. Among those in the front are Lt Peter Beach, Lt Jack Richards and Sgt Reg Luscombe.

Ottery St Mary Home Guard parade through the town in 1941.

Officers and NCOs of No. 4 Platoon (Axminster) B Company 19th (Seaton) Battalion, Devon Home Guard. Back row, left to right: Cpl W. Dixon, L/Cpl T. March, L/Cpl J. Hayball, Sgt O. Chapple, Cpl J. Meniss, L/Cpl F. Manley, Cpl S. Wench, Cpl E. Parker. Middle: L/Cpl D. Venn, L/Cpl W. Manley, L/Cpl J. Board, Sgt A. Henry, L/Cpl R. Bird, L/Cpl C. Gapper, Cpl A. Perham, Sgt T. Wilson. Front: 2nd Lt A. Hayter, 2nd Lt J. Potter, 2nd Lt C. Cross, Lt J. Wraight, Lt D. Snell, CSM T. Young, 2nd Lt L. Hill, 2nd Lt E. Bridle.

Exeter Home Guard on parade in the High Street in 1942. Note the anti-blast wall in front of the Guildhall.

Uplyme Home Guard at their stand-down parade in the old village hall in 1945. The Home Guard was formed as the LDV (Local Defence Volunteers) in the wake of Dunkirk, when a German invasion was more than a possibility. Uplyme's 'Dad's Army' were due to visit a local rifle range on 8 May 1945 but the arrival of VE Day made this superfluous, and they trooped off to a nearby quarry and celebrated in style firing off all their ammunition. Among members seen here are Alf Hurst, Bill Crabb, Len Copp, John Turner, Mr Fisher, Jim Curtis, Bill Cross, Tom Sloman, Charlie Slade, Hubert Samways, the two Collier brothers, Fred Peach, Lionel Fisher, Len Copp, John Currall, Billy Stone and Fred Kingman.

Ted Lewis (left) on parade with members of Chardstock Home Guard in 1942. The village cricket club had its pavilion commandeered by the Home Guard, who dismantled and re-erected it at Storridge Lane where it served as a look-out and a store hut. It never survived the war, the cricketers purchasing an army-surplus bell tent to serve as a temporary pavilion when the club restarted in 1947.

Farway Home Guard, c. 1943. Back row, left to right: Roger Wood, Harry Batten, Jack Webber, Cedric Summers, Ernie Baily, Tom Spurway. Second row: Sam Reed, Brian Lane, Nick Reed, Jack Batten, ? Sweetland, -?-, Bob Summers, Wilfred Payne. Third row: Sam Lane, Jim Price, Bob Newbery, ? Parris, Gordon Snell, Tony Tett, Tom Berry. Front: Geoff Norman, Philip Mitchell, Albert Sweetland, Fred Holland, Leonard Millhead, George Tucker, Jack Spiller, Ern Goddard.

Axminster members of B Company, 19th (Seaton) Battalion, Devon Home Guard, on parade at Axminster on 16 May 1943. Left to right are Harry Cawley, Col Cutter, -?-, General Newman.

Offwell Home Guard, c. 1943. Among members seen here are Percy Heard, Nelson Bessell, Bill Wilson, Cedric Somers, Ern Bright, Harry and Eric Stamp, Jack Hole, Bob Newbery, Bill Parris, Perce Harding and Messrs Chick, Baily, Hutchings, Lane, Batten and the Pearce brothers. One of their watch-points was Bishop's Tower, where the men slept when on duty (although it leaked!). In 1944, when England's defence during the D-Day preparations devolved on the Home Guard, their duties included guarding Honiton Tunnel with a platoon completed by telephonists, runners and a first aid party. In case of attack, men were entrenched at either end of the tunnel, and double lines of field telephone laid to connect the Platoon HQ. Reserves were arranged from both the US troops at Heathfield Camp and the Honiton Home Guard. These duties were between 24 April and 10 July and involved a total of 11,000 attendances.

Membury Home Guard around 1944. On the extreme left is Captain Williams; other members include Major Russell, Lt George Ashley, George Bradfield, Frank Davey and Stan Wakley.

Membury Home Guard, c. 1943. Back row, left to right: Fred Beeching, ? Shepherd, Harold Newbery, Bill Pitman, Bill Hartnell. Middle: Bill Down, Eric Marks, Eric Knight, Arthur Cleal, Bert Thomas, Reg Legg, Bill Thomas, John Knight, Denis Pitman, Roy Manley, Cecil Fowler, Art Penecard, Seymour Dunn, Fred Smith, Ned Bailey, Les Bradfield, Marwood Ashley. Front: Jack Long, Norman Ellis, Ern Sloman, Stan Wakley, George Ashley, Frank Davey, Archie Gale, Charlie Wood, Sam Davey, Dickie Bird.

Honiton's mayor, Alderman Fred Studley, inspects the local Home Guard units at Allhallows Playing Fields, Honiton, on 16 May 1943.

Luppitt Home Guard pose outside the pavilion at the Allhallows Playing Fields, Honiton, prior to their standing down parade on 31 December 1944. Back row, left to right: Geoff Spiller, Syd Valentine, Len Drew, Charles Crabb, Ken Pulman, Albie Wright, -?-, Charles Coles, Walter Ayres, Bill Blackmore, Jack Middleton, Capt Rock, Gilbert Clapp, Edgar Thorn, Walter Manville, Dan Buck, John Wilson, Eli Loveridge, Syd Middleton, Ralph Rosewell, Walter Hart. Front: Jack Thorne, Carl Churchill, Sam Ewins, Tom Martin, Albie Crabb, Jack Sage, Bill Walden, Wilf Parkins, ? Edwards, Arthur Braddick, Fred Braddick, Archie Corrick, George Hooper.

The 1st (Loyal City of Exeter) Battalion, Devon Home Guard were the first Home Guard battalion to have their own flag and are thought to have been the only battalion to have their own flag when the Home Guard was 'Stood Down' on 31 December 1944. The flag had been the brainchild of a Lt E.A.R. King of No. 1 Company and, with the wholehearted support of Major H.J. Wilsher, second-in-command, permission was sought from Gen. Sir Charles Maynard, Colonel, the Devonshire Regiment, who agreed, suggesting that the flag bear the crest of the Devonshire Regiment. The Mayor and Corporation of the City (of Exeter) said that the Civic Authorities would be pleased to present a flag to the Battalion. The presentation, seen above, took place at a parade on 16 May 1943 to mark the third anniversary of the Home Guard. It was held at the County Ground at St Thomas, Exeter. During the war the flag was only taken out for ceremonial parades, and after the war the flag was handed over to the Mayor for safe custody.

The flag of the 1st (Loyal City of Exeter) Battalion, Exeter Home Guard.

Members of the 22 Devon (5th SR) Battalion Home Guard with a lady member, Queenie Pring (now Mrs Retter), who was attached to the 5th Home Guard Battalion as a typist to Lt-Col A.H. Greening, the battalion commander, and Captain Taylor, the adjutant. Her place of duty was in an office near the Clock Tower. Front row, left to right: Queenie Pring, Major Baker, company commander, Captain Taylor, Lt-Col Greening, Captain Jones, Sam Floyd.

Lt Dick Snell and members of No.1 (Uplyme) Platoon, 19th (Seaton) Battalion, Home Guard Devonshire Regiment, on parade at Latches, Axminster, in May 1943.

Woodbury Home Guard, c. 1943. Back row, left to right: L/Cpl Gooding, Ptes Morrish, Baker, Down, Bowles, Blackmore, Miller, Brewer, Goss, Skinner, Yeo, L/Cpl Jarman, Mrs Lowman. Second row: Mrs Wright, Ptes Palmer, Stamp, Baker, Tucker, Stubbs, Auton, Edworthy, Hawkins, Ridler, L/Cpl Middleton, Ptes Williams, Sharland. Third row: Mrs Brewer, Mrs Morrish, Mrs Grey, L/Cpl Boyland, Cpl Wilson, Sgt Smith, Sgt Gallienne, Sgt Lowman, Lt Rickeard, Lt Pavey, QSM Chattock, Sgt Tapley, Sgt Hollet, Cpl Smith, Cpl Marks, Mr Daw (signal master), Mrs Daw, Miss Fulford. Front: Ptes Reeves (DR), Armstrong, Sellick, Marks, Newton, Hitchcock, Bamsey, Chapman, Radford, Hawkins, Pavey (DR).

Exeter Home Guard members, October 1944, on the banks of the River Exe at Exeter Quay. Major Greenslade (front centre) lived at Exwick village; Lt Thomas Powell, standing on the extreme left, was living in Okehampton Road at the time; seated second left is Lt Hunt from Cowick Lane, who ran a decorating business.

Axminster members of the 19th (Seaton) Battalion, Home Guard Devonshire Regiment, on a firing range at Marsh Farm, Kilmington. Judging by the fact that many of the men present are not in uniform it is possible that the picture was taken soon after the formation of the LDV in 1940. Here Lt S.O. Gill (the well-known Axminster baker) demonstrates the finer points of a weapon to Lt Dick Snell.

No. 4 Platoon (Axminster) B Company, 19th (Seaton) Battalion, Devon Home Guard at its 'Stand Down' Parade in Axminster Square on 3 December 1944. The Home Guard were formed following an appeal on 19 May 1940 by the War Minister, Mr Anthony Eden, for units to be formed to resist a possible invasion by the Germans who were advancing rapidly through France and Belgium. The following morning, Lord Sidmouth, as Chairman of the Honiton RDC, called a meeting of regular retired officers resident in the neighbourhood, with the chairman of the local branch of the British Legion, to organize the recruitment of volunteers.

Arrangements were made to form a Honiton Company with platoons at Broadhembury, Upottery, Honiton and Feniton. Similar action was taken at Seaton, and anti-tank obstacles were placed along the promenade. Outlying platoons were formed at Rousdon, Colyton and Branscombe. At Axminster a company was formed with platoons at Axminster, Uplyme, Yarcombe, Kilmington, Chardstock and Hawkchurch. In the early stages, an East Devon Group was formed, including the units from Exeter to the Dorset border. The original Honiton Battalion proved too large for a single command, and the personnel were distributed into the 19th (Seaton) Battalion, and the Clyst Battalion, under a group commander. Members are seen below during a wartime parade.

Five
WW2 – Civil Defence

Rescue workers in Paris Street, Exeter, after the 1942 raids.

The Cathedral Church of St Peter in Exeter has looked out over nearly 800 years of the city's history, never more violent than in 1942 when the Luftwaffe returned for its second attack in a week. On 4 May the Cathedral received a direct hit, that badly damaged the chapel of St James and its Muniment Room and crypt, together with the South Quire Aisle. All the magnificent glass was shattered, although the medieval glass and other treasures had been taken away to a place of safety, and the organ was wrecked. Restoration was a long and costly affair.

Blitzed Bamfylde Street, Exeter, 1942.

The Cross, looking towards Chapel Street, Exmouth, after the air raid in January 1941.

Although the Cathedral was the aiming point for Exeter's city centre, not all the bombers were that accurate. This massive crater resulted from a bomb dropped on Burnthouse Lane.

Exeter's Lower Market was destroyed in the 1942 raids. The city's post-war reconstruction plans did not allow for its rebuilding, and shops and new streets cover the site.

Along with Bath, York, Norwich and Canterbury, Exeter was selected from English cities listed in Karl Baedeker's well-known guide books, which gave their name to the 'Baedeker Raids'. These were 'revenge' raids for RAF attacks on German cities, notably the Baltic Hansa town of Lubeck and its neighbour Rostock. The Luftwaffe Inspector-General Erhard Milch is said to have suggested attacking similar English targets and the guide books were checked to find suitable cities. Unfortunately for Exeter, it was the first chosen, and the first of two main raids was carried out on the night of 23-24 April 1942. Much damage was done around the Cathedral, notably in Dix's Field, Southernhay and Bedford Circus. The bombers returned on 3-4 May to eviscerate much of the city centre, Fore Street, High Street, South Street and Sidwell Street which is seen above and unrecognisable as today's busy shopping centre. Around two thousand houses were destroyed, even more were damaged, and there were around a thousand casualties, two hundred and fifty of them fatal.

Cathedral School, Exeter, after the 1942 raids.

Like most English cities with bombed sites, Exeter used many of them for car parks during the reconstruction period. This shows the east side of Bedford Street in June 1951. Off centre to the right is Catherine Street, with Colson's (now Dingle's) shop well advertised.

Post-war reconstruction of Exeter was slow, largely because of shortages of building materials of all kinds. Sidwell Street in December 1953 still has plenty of gaps.

Deller's Café in Bedford Street was one of Exeter's best-loved landmarks. It was built between 1912 and 1916 with what some thought an out-of-character Baroque entrance. It was virtually destroyed in the 1942 raids and later pulled down. Sadly no longer part of Exeter's life, Dellers restarted with a café in High Street and a cafeteria in Paul Street.

Post-war reconstruction included a new road from Bedford Street, being constructed here in 1956.

Post-war reconstruction work in Bedford Circus, 1952. The Devon & Exeter Savings Bank is today's TSB.

Exeter firemen with the engine they took to help fight the fires at Bristol during that city's bombing in 1940. Maurice England is centre front.

A fire crew outside the old fire station in New North Road, Exeter, *c.* 1941. Stan Shepherd is on right.

Bomb disposal squad members at Danes Castle, Exeter, around 1942.

Membury Civil Defence Corps during World War Two. Back row, left to right: Mr Batten, Bill Harvey, Jim Denslow. Front row: Mr Priest, Tom Knight.

Exeter members of the NFS (National Fire Service) passing Whitbread's High Street shop during the the city's 1945 Victory Parade in May.

Many Exeter residents worked night time with the civil defence forces, including these nurses from the Royal Devon & Exeter Hospital who formed the hospital's fire-fighting squad.

Six

WW2 – Keep the Home Fires Burning

Land Army girls at work near Honiton around 1943.

Any material that could be re-used or recycled was collected and precious shipping space saved for other purposes. Here Branscombe boys and girls collect waste paper. Above, left to right: W. Trivett, Edith Self, Eric Pauley, Joyce Frappell and Doris Whatten at the back, Henry Adlam, Morrie Ward, Henry Carpenter. Below: Betty Somers, Florrie Bateman, Joyce Whatten and Eileen Batten pause for a well-earned breather.

Opposite: To a beleaguered nation fighting for its life, and with every inch of cargo space at a premium on the convoys making the dangerous Atlantic crossing, salvage drives in every town and village played an important part in making the munitions that kept Britain's war efforts going. Nothing was spared. Church railings, handsome and ornate gates that would warrant preservation orders today, saucepans, treasured letters, valuable books, old postcards, and the day-to-day waste including papers, packets, tins. The Scouting (and Guiding) movement played its part with members working hard in collection and at sorting depots. In Devon a 'handsome silver cup' was presented by the Waste Paper Recovery Association. The school which collected the largest amount of waste paper in a month had its name engraved on it and then held it for a month.

74

SAVE PAPER

and help to win the War

This Handsome Silver Cup to be Presented

"FOR VICTORY"
Presented by the WASTE PAPER RECOVERY ASSOC in recognition of very valuable services in the collection of Salvage for Munitions of War

MARCH 1948 DEVON DEVON SCHOOL

OUR COUNTRY NEEDS every scrap of waste paper, so see that none is wasted in your home! Bring it to school — the old newspapers, the cardboard cartons and boxes, your old story books and magazines — and your school will not only be helping the War effort but will also be able to compete for this HANDSOME SILVER CUP. The school in your area which collects the largest amount of waste paper in a month will hold the cup for this period and it's name will be engraved on it! Ask your teacher about this grand scheme whereby you can all help to win the War.

QUESTIONS YOU ARE ASKING.

WHY is paper so urgently needed ? — BECAUSE it makes so many parts for munitions.

WHY is there a shortage of paper ? — BECAUSE so much of it comes from abroad.

WHY can't we bring enough from abroad ? — BECAUSE we need the ships to carry the food, troops, planes, tanks and for other vital purposes.

SO IT'S UP TO YOU AND YOUR SCHOOLFELLOWS!

Don't waste paper – bring it to School

ONE OLD NEWSPAPER	ONE OLD MAGAZINE	ONE OLD SOAP POWDER TIN	SIX OLD BOOKS	TWELVE OLD LETTERS
WILL MAKE PARTS FOR **THREE SHELLS**	WILL MAKE PARTS FOR **TWO MINES**	WILL MAKE PARTS FOR **FOUR AERO ENGINES**	WILL MAKE A CARRIER FOR **MORTAR SHELLS**	WILL MAKE A BOX FOR **RIFLE CARTRIDGES**

Members of the Women's Land Army were stationed at Fairview, Honiton, during World War Two and, after an interim reunion in 1974 at the Angel, held a 50th Anniversary Reunion at Honiton Motel on 11 July 1992 (below) to which former members came from all over England. Above at Fairview around 1944 can be see Mary Kehoe, Joyce Marsden, Jean Gordon, Vera Tanner, Dolly Wilkes (the hostel warden), Paulene Bowden, Florrie Bailey, Kath Allen, Agnes Wardle and Doreen Wilson.

Violet Blackmore (left) and Dorothy Bending, two Ottery St Mary girls who 'did their bit' by joining the Land Army during World War Two.

Women from all walks of life joined the Land Army and learnt all sorts of new skills. This one, seen on a farm near Honiton, is thatching a hayrick.

Branscombe Special Constables, 1940. Left to right: Archie Perryman, Harry Lazell, Percy Perryman, Bert Somers, Len Dowell.

Many factories moved out of London, either as a safety precaution or, as was the case with Shands at Axminster, because they had been bombed out. Nestlés Munitions arrived at Branscombe from Holloway in London. Their factory, seen here around 1946, is in the foreground, with Margells Hill and Millers Lea behind.

Exeter Gas Board staff were evacuated to Topsham after their offices at Southernhay were destroyed in 1942.

The exchange of plaques between Alderman Fred Studley (Honiton's mayor) and Lt-Commander Brembridge RN at Honiton's Navy Week in May 1943.

British Restaurants were opened in many towns during World War Two, their purpose being to provide hot meals outside rationing restrictions at reasonable prices (for a shilling you could get a roast dinner). Honiton's British Restaurant in the Pannier Market was opened on 2 May 1943 by the Mayor and Mayoress, Alderman F. and Mrs E.M. Studley. Here Mrs Studley is being served with the first meal. Below, enjoying their meals are, left to right, Mr Coates, the town clerk, the Mayor, Revd J.E.L. Logan, Mayor's Chaplain, the Mayoress. Those in the background include Mr Hatcher, Mr B. Turney and Mrs Davey.

Budleigh Salterton's 'Salute the Soldier Week' in 1944 saw the town's £75,000 target supplemented by £5,000 targets for East Budleigh and Otterton. The week began on Saturday 20 May with a 'Parade of the Fighting Forces of Great Britain and the United States of America', many of whom would be landing in Normandy in less than three weeks time.

The opening of Exeter's 'Salute The Soldier Week' took place with a backdrop reminder that there was a war on. The city easily passed its £750,000 target.

Feeding time in the piggery at the Women's Land Army Training Unit at Whimple in 1944.

Hitler was probably wise not to invade England: he would have had a severe 'hand-bagging' if the determined looks on these ladies' faces are anything to go by. They are all regulars of the Duke of York pub in Sidwell Street and are pictured here immediately after the 1942 blitz.

82

Exeter postwomen during World War Two.

Women's Land Army Training School at Whimple House, Whimple, in 1944. Girls who had completed their training pose with regular staff at the centre.

Honiton's Civil Defence Corps' new rescue van arrives in the town with Mr Proll at the wheel.

Axminster Observer Corp at the Observation Post just off Lyme Road, *c.* 1943. Back row, left to right: -?-, -?-, Mr Harding, -?-, Arthur McNeil, Howard Sutton, Mark Hooper, -?-. Front: Albert Trivett, -?-, Jack Gosling, Bert Perham, -?-, Gordon Gapper, Herbert Mearing.

Warners Holiday Camp (now Haven Holidays) in Seaton was used for various purposes during World War Two, housing internees and, later, the American forces preparing for D-Day. In the earlier years it was also used as a POW camp, mainly for Italian soldiers, many of whom volunteered to work on various farms in East Devon including, shown here, Home Farm on the Rousdon estate. Above, Tom Gapper is left and Stan Carter right, with POWs. The difference in status, if any, between those wearing triangular trouser patches and the ones with circular patches is not known. Below, the cart horse joins in the posing.

Exeter firewomen on parade in High Street in 1941.

The Home Secretary, Mr Herbert Morrison, inspects the National Fire Service (NFS) at Honiton on 31 December 1942. Here he speaks to the Mayor, Alderman Fred Studley. Town Clerk Mr W. Beer is behind.

The opening of the ATS Recruiting Centre in Honiton's High Street by Mayor Alderman F. Studley in May 1943. Town Clerk Mr Coates in on his right.

In the wake of the spontaneous celebrations in the shape of street parties that followed World War Two, more organised services of thanksgiving were held throughout the land. Budleigh Salterton's took place on The Green in 1945.

Exeter Air Training Corp Band head a church parade through a blitzed High Street during World War Two. The drum major is John Bastone.

The wedding of Mary Elizabeth Trenchard of Axminster to Richard Todd of Charlotte, North Carolina, USA, at St Mary's church, Axminster, in 1944.

GIs were not the only ones to find romance abroad. Bill Finnemore, from Uplyme though born in the USA to an American mother, served before and during World War Two in India, where he met and married Thelma Roots. Bill, a warrant officer in the Royal Army Medical Corp, and Thelma are seen here after their wedding at St Teresa's church in Calcutta, India, in December 1945. Bill brought his bride home to Uplyme where they lived until Bill's death in 1996.

The wedding of Cpl Milferd Green, a Californian with the 315th Station Hospital at Axminster, and Axminster girl Joan Chubb on 4 December 1944. Left to right: Margory Staddon, Kenneth McKnight (best man), Sylvia Young, Milferd Green, Joan Chubb, Kathleen Chubb, Walter Chubb, Jean Mounter. The best man later married Sylvia Young. Milferd Green visited Axminster on his Golden Wedding anniversary. He went to the site of the American Hospital, now the Millwey Rise housing estate, and was saddened that there is no trace of the former camp or plaque recording its existence. He died a few months later.

No. 5 First Aid Post was based at Buddle Lane Community Centre, Exeter, where they soon gained a name for efficiency, as evidenced here by the Inter-First Aid Post championship shield in 1943.

Specially trained workers at the main entrance of the University College of the South West (now the Exeter and Devon Arts Centre) in Gandy Street, Exeter, in November 1940. They were recruited by the Ministry of Labour to repair fighter aircraft damaged in combat or crashes. Work was carried out on wings at Pike's Garage in Alphington Street (later the Plaza) and on fuselages at the Blackboy Road bus station. Then the parts were taken out to Exeter aerodrome, assembled and flown back to their squadrons.

VE Day Fancy Dress Party at St Katherine's Road, Exeter, May 1945.

VE Day Party at Poltimore Square, Exeter, in 1945. Today the square is the site of the King William Street car park. Then it had its own air raid shelter into which the children were taken when the siren sounded.

Some people were still celebrating the end of World War Two a year later. Male regulars of the Wonford Inn pose before their Victory Outing in 1946.

The Avenue, Exmouth, held its VJ Day Party in St Mary's Church Hall (since demolished). Enjoying themselves here are Mr and Mrs Coles and their children, Grace and Dorothy, Mr and Mrs and Rita Parker, Peter, David and Ivy Gillard, Mr and Mrs Yool, Reg Gillard, Mrs Hine, Vi Dowell, Mr and Mrs Crang and Mr and Mrs and Joan Tyler.

The VE Day Party on the lawn of
Church House, Sidmouth, saw all the
children wearing brightly coloured
rosettes in patriotic colours. Among
those present are Kay Solman, Mrs
Govier, Gordon Dunsford, John
Govier, Sidmouth's vicar, the Revd
Ball, Maureen Drewer, Nurse Chalker,
Lilly Harris, and Sheila Robinson.

VE Day celebrations in Charles Street, Exmouth, with well-known character Romeo Reynolds
on the extreme right with his barrel organ. Among those present are Miss Elsie Fisher, Mrs
Perriam, Mrs Murch, Mr and Mrs Back and their nieces, Mrs Polly Fisher, Rita Miller and her
mother (later, as Mrs Ball, landlady of the First and Last Inn in Exmouth), Mrs Hayes, Mrs
Richards, Mrs Stuart, Mrs French and Mrs Smith.

VE Day celebrations in Sandhill Street, Ottery St Mary, on 8 May 1945. Among those present are Sid Salter, Mrs Totterdell and Milly Loveless. The three ladies seated front right are probably from London.

Standing, left to right: Sid Salter, Josie Salter. The front row includes Mrs Padden, Maud Berry (with jug), Mr 'Stumpy' Carter and Mary Hele. Among the children are some evacuees.

Seven

WW2 – 'Thin Red Line of 'Eroes'

Exeter Shell Factory, 1916. The Princess Royal talks with members of the ATS at Exeter during a West Country tour in July 1941.

Evacuation from Swancombe in Kent to Shermoor House near Broadclyst Station in 1939 was to have a profound affect on seven-year-old Joy Wallis. Seen below with her brother Trevor and mother Doris in around 1940, she returned to Broadclyst at the age of 17 and met Colin Seward, her future husband. The families had been friendly during the Wallis's time in the village, Mrs Wallis helping out at the village store which was run by Mrs Seward. As Joy Seward, the one-time evacuee girl and her husband joined the family business to help run the popular Kingswood Hotel on Sidmouth's Esplanade and have been doing so for forty years. They are pictured above in 1952.

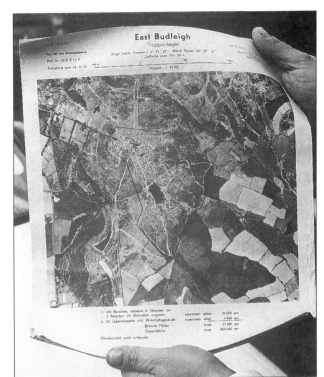

German reconnaissance pilots took this shot of East Budleigh in 1942 (it is not clear whether the date '24.4.42' is of the photograph or of its printing). With due respect to Sir Walter Raleigh's birthplace and its Home Guard, one wonders at the military importance of this small East Devon village.

Gladys Pile (in the middle of the back row, then Gladys Middleton), now living at Park Close, Woodbury, had never been further than Taunton when she set off for Droitwich in 1942 to join the ATS and was posted to Blandford Forum and the 564 Battalion of the 183rd AA Regiment. Her wartime experiences included a posting to Kent in time for action against the V1 flying bombs (the 'Doodlebugs') and being shelled from France whilst near Ramsgate and Margate. Then it was off for Belgium where she spent VE Day. Gladys was demobbed in 1946 when she returned to Woodbury and life as a farmer's wife.

Unlike the picture on the previous page, there is no need to wonder at the wartime importance of this map bearing the date 24.4.42, the day after Exeter's first heavy raid. It is of Exeter Aerodrome (Flugplatz). Clyst Honiton and its church can plainly be seen towards the bottom. Running from top to bottom and roughly parallel are the A30 trunk road and the Waterloo–Exeter main line.

Stan Gudge of Uplyme joined the 4th Devons Territorial Battalion in January 1940 at Buller Institute, Plymouth, and was soon posted overseas to Gibraltar where he served until 1943. He then served in the United Kingdom until being demobbed in February 1946 as a sergeant. In 1943 he married his childhood sweetheart Stephanie Holdway, who had volunteered for service with the WAAF (later WRAF) in March 1941 and with whom she served until September 1945, being stationed at RAF Mountbatten (Plymouth), Thorney Island and Pembroke Dock. The couple still live in Uplyme where Stephanie still treasures all of their many letters written during the five years they were separated.

The duty crew waiting for visiting aircraft at RAF Exeter in 1941 includes Exeter man Don Richards (left front). Exeter City Council acquired the land at Honiton Clyst for Exeter Airport in 1936. It started as a 90-acre grass airfield, its first airliner flight being in 1937 from Jersey. It trebled in size during the war when it was requisitioned by the Air Ministry for use as a fighter station. Today it belongs to Devon County Council.

Arnheim veterans at the first showing of the film *Theirs Is The Glory* at the Gaumont Cinema, Exeter, in 1945, are greeted outside the cinema by civic leaders. The film was about the battle later featured in *A Bridge Too Far*. Third left (in uniform) is Tom Symons. The American naval officers in the background were stationed in Exeter at the time.

Like most of the South Coast, East Devon was filled with constructions aimed at defence in the event of invasion. Pill boxes, strong points, lines of tank obstacles and barbed wire mushroomed. Some remain to this day. The Axe Valley, an obvious route inland for invaders, was especially 'defended'. Outside the Trout Inn in Chard Road, Axminster (now closed), was a slotted, concrete block; its 'twin' was on the opposite side of the road in the garden of a now-demolished cottage (left). If German tanks drove up the hill out of Axminster, a length of railway track would be slid through the slots to bar the road. Happily, especially for the Home Guard who might have had to fit the rails, the tanks never arrived.

For obvious reasons, pictures of invasion defences are far from common. The row of tank traps that were to be found on all sea fronts can still be seen in this 1946 postcard from Branscombe. The barbed wire that festooned them has been removed but the pill box behind the tea shanty still stands guard.

The threat of invasion was very real during the summer of 1940 and the entire South Coast was covered with barbed wire and tank obstacles. For obvious reasons sea fronts received extra attention, as can be seen from this picture of Budleigh Salterton in around 1940. There were also secondary lines of defence. Once those barriers had been breached German tanks would have found their way inland barred by concrete 'tank traps' of the type seen below at the entrance to Budleigh's Fore Street.

Sea defences at Budleigh Salterton included this light gun at the top of Coastguard Hill. Manned here by the Home Guard, it had supporting fire from a Lewis Gun.

An army convoy, including this tank transporter, enters South Street, Exeter, from Fore Street in around 1943.

Cecil Sansom had a varied war. One of the low points came early on when he was posted to his home town of Axminster and billeted in what had once been Fred Ball's harness makers shop in Trinity Square. When a particularly humourless Sgt 'Topper' Brown discovered Cecil lived a few yards around the corner at his parents' fish and chip and wet fish shop in South Street, he took particular delight in marching him (and the rest of the squad) along South Street and putting them through a lengthy arms drill outside the shop. Cecil had joined up on 28 August 1939 in D Company Devonshire Regiment Territorial Army and was transferred to the Young Soldiers Battalion (70th Gloucesters) when his mother wrote to tell the War Office that he put his age on in order to volunteer. He went back to the 12th Devons for spells at Exmouth and then with Bren Gun Carrier Platoon at Widworthy Court, near Honiton.

This was followed by that spell at Axminster and then another on the Isle of Wight. His older brother Ken 'claimed' him for the 6th Battalion, Royal Sussex Regiment, at Crowborough (older brothers could claim younger brothers, i.e. have them transferred to their unit). Cecil finally went to the Middle East, where he volunteered to join the newly-formed SBS (Special Boat Unit). This led to his parachuting behind enemy lines in Greece and Yugoslavia. One such drop ended with his being caught in a tree in pitch darkness with no idea how far below the ground was. Unable to drop free for fear of breaking a leg, he waited some hours in the cold and dark before seeing lights approaching. It was not the Germans but partisans looking for him – and he was only four feet off the ground! He went to Italy, where he saw Mussolini and his mistress strung up in Milan. Service with the Chindits in Burma was to follow but the Hiroshima bomb intervened and he stayed home. On 23 October 1945 he married Miss Kathleen Sene from Wonford, Exeter, whom he had met before her service with the WRAF (1941-45).

The George and Dragon at Clyst St George was a popular haunt of fighter pilots at RAF Exeter (now Exeter Airport) and they began a tradition of autographing the bar ceiling as seen here. A move after the war to have the inn's sign changed to an RAF pilot St George slaying a Luftwaffe dragon was not continued with when some objected on the grounds that the war was over and bygones should be bygones. Silly people.

American servicemen soon discovered the attractions of English pubs like the George and Dragon. The airmen seen here in around 1944 were stationed at RAF Exeter.

Joe Capozzie (left) and fellow GI Salestrone Cataliotti were billeted with the Bottomley family in Alphington Road, Exeter, in 1943. They are seen here with the Bottomleys' son Peter.

Generally speaking, AA patrolmen were placed in the Military Police if they joined the Services in World War Two; their RAC counterparts went into the RAF. Bill Snell, seen on the left at RAF Brize Norton, had been the RAC's man for the stretch of road from Fairmile through Honiton to Devonshire Inn before the war, and because RAC patrolmen had received first aid training he became a crash ambulance driver. Joining in 1939, he served in SEAC (India) and Egypt before demobilization as a Flight Sergeant in 1945. On his return he became the landlord of the Three Tuns Inn in Honiton's High Street.

Members of Sidbury Home Guard, c. 1941, about to set off on a dawn patrol around the hills that surround this picturesque village to see if any parachutists had landed during the night. The handsome Armstrong-Siddely car, one of the first automatics, was specially purchased for the job. Left to right: Sgt 'Bunny' Palmer, Lt Strickland, Pte W. Pike, Cpl D. Finlayson.

Not a nightmare-sized New Age travellers' camp, but an aerial view of the Hawkerland Valley Supply Area between Newton Poppleford and Exeter (the then A35 road climbs out of Newton Poppleford towards Woodbury Common in the right background). Seen here on 12 December 1944, it was the stores depot for the USAAF's Fleet Air Wing Seven at Dunkeswell.

Polish members of the RAF march past the Mayor of Exeter, Mr R. Glover-Saunders, as they parade to Exeter Cathedral during World War Two. Below, they line up for inspection outside the Cathedral.

Flt-Lt Frank Rowe of Axminster receiving his pilot's wings from Brigadier Daniels at Petersborough, Port Alfred, South Africa, on 18 February 1944. Frank, who is well known in Axminster's sporting and business life, trained as a pilot on Avro Ansons and later flew the famous Avro Lancaster bombers.

Bob Ferguson was a veteran of Dunkirk and later saw action in North Africa and India, staying on in the army until 1982. He finished his wartime service commanding a Royal Engineers Unit clearing Britain's south coast of beach mines. During the war he was billeted at Ottery St Mary, in Otter Switchgear's factory, and it was there that he met his wife-to-be, Ivy, who worked in the local Food Office and helped out with ARP duties at night. They were married in June 1945, Ivy having to save up clothing coupons to buy her wedding outfit. They are seen here just before leaving for their honeymoon at Babbacombe. Retiring to Ottery St Mary, Bob became a popular councillor with both Ottery's parish council and the East Devon District Council.

Axminster-born Richard Gordon 'Dick' Sweetland joined up in June 1940, serving in the 12th (Airborne) Battalion Devon Regiment, with whom, as a parachutist, he had the unusual experience of arriving in Normandy on D+1 by landing craft. Later he was among the first British troops to cross the Rhine, doing so by boat. During the very early days of the Normandy campaign Dick was largely responsible for the production in the front line of the first issue of what became the *Swedebasher*, a front-line newspaper for the troops that continued after the war as the mouthpiece for former members of the 12th Devons who kept in touch through it and the many reunions it inspired. Dick was to be its editor for forty-two years, and this work led to his receiving the BEM in the New Year Honours list on 1 January 1987. His work on the Axminster Rural District Council led to his moving to Sidmouth in 1974 when local government reorganisation saw the formation of the East Devon District Council. He died in 1994.

Pont Tournat (above) and Pegasus Bridge (below) were important bridges that needed to be captured early on D-Day in order to facilitate the speedy movement inland of the main British and Canadian forces. The bridges and the gliders used in their capture are see here on D-Day. Pegasus Bridge, especially, has become part of the folklore of the whole campaign.

Sergeant-Major Bernard Hiscox, Royal Marines, was decorated for bravery at Buckingham Palace by King George VI in November 1945. The award was 'for leadership, courage, and zeal shown in HM LCF4 during the successful landings at Salerno (Italy) in September 1943'. Bernard joined the Royal Marines in 1940 and took part in twenty-eight operations against the enemy, including the ill-fated Dieppe operation. He served in North and South America, India, Burma, North Africa, Italy, Yugoslavia, France, Greece and Egypt. As a middleweight boxer he represented the naval boxing team for Sicily and Italy. On his return to Axminster he played in goal, with considerable ability, for the Town football club.

" Pulman's Weekly News,"
November 27th, 1945.

AXMINSTER.

DECORATED WITH THE D.S.M.

SERGT. BERNARD HISCOX AT THE
PALACE.

Sergt. Bernard M. Hiscox, Royal
Marines, of Silver-street, Axminster,
attended an investiture at Buckingham Palace on Tuesday, when he
received from the King the Distin-
guished Service Medal. He was accom-
panied by his wife Mrs. Joan Hiscox,
and his mother. Mrs. Matthew Hiscox,
of Castle Hill, Axminster.

It was in May, 1944, that the
" London Gazette " published the
award of the D.S.M. to Sergt Hiscox
" for leadership, courage, and zeal
shown in H.M L.C F.4 (landing craft
flak) in operations which led to successful landings at Salerno in September, 1943 " He then held the rank
of Acting-Sergeant-Major.

Joining the Marines in February,
1940. Sergt Hiscox took part in 28
operations against the enemy, including 14 H-hour D-Day landings, begin-
ning with the Dieppe raid in August,
1942 His service took him to both
Americas, India, Burma, Africa, Italy,
Yugoslavia, France, Greece, and
Egypt. His campaign ribbons are the
1939-45 Star, Atlantic Star, France
and Germany Star Africa Star and
clasp and Italy Star.

A middle-weight boxer, he was a
representative of the Naval Boxing
Team for Sicily and Italy in 1943 and
1944 Sergt Hiscox was discharged
a week before his investiture, and
has resumed his civilian occupation
as a weaver with Axminster Carpets,
Ltd

The extract from *Pulman's Weekly News* of 27 November 1945 which gave details of Bernard Hiscox's decoration at Buckingham Palace (see opposite).

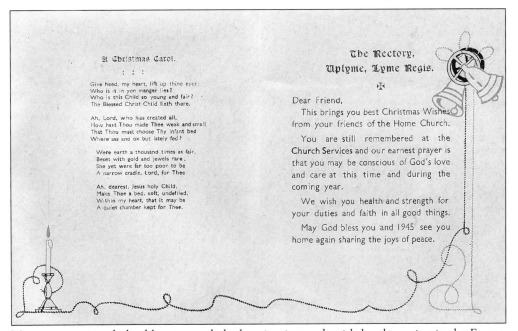

A Christmas Carol.

Give heed, my heart, lift up thine eyes:
Who is it in yon manger lies?
Who is this Child so young and fair?
The Blessed Christ Child lieth there.

Ah, Lord, who has created all,
How hast Thou made Thee weak and small
That Thou must choose Thy infant bed
Where ass and ox but lately fed?

Were earth a thousand times as fair,
Beset with gold and jewels rare,
She yet were far too poor to be
A narrow cradle, Lord, for Thee

Ah, dearest, Jesus holy Child,
Make Thee a bed, soft, undefiled,
Within my heart, that it may be
A quiet chamber kept for Thee.

The Rectory,
Uplyme, Lyme Regis.

Dear Friend,
This brings you best Christmas Wishes from your friends of the Home Church.

You are still remembered at the Church Services and our earnest prayer is that you may be conscious of God's love and care at this time and during the coming year.

We wish you health and strength for your duties and faith in all good things.

May God bless you and 1945 see you home again sharing the joys of peace.

Most communities helped boost morale by keeping in touch with locals serving in the Forces, especially those overseas. Christmas cards, such as that sent here from Uplyme in 1944 by a committee formed for that purpose through the church, were popular.

Stan Davis of Axminster (above, third from left at the back) at Corfe Castle Camp in 1939, were he was serving with the Devonshire Regiment TA. He later became attached to General (later Field Marshall) Montgomery's personal staff as a driver and was present at Luneberg Heath in Germany on 4 May 1945 when General Jodl surrendered all enemy forces in Northern Europe. General Montgomery is seen below receiving the German delegates prior to the signing of the instrument of surrender.

Eight
Peacetime Wars

Axminster Victory Celebrations Committee.
WELCOME HOME FUND

Axminster,
November 9th, 1946

Dear Sir or Madam,

    During the war the people at home sent Christmas greetings and a small gift each year to all you Axminster men and women who were on active service. It was decided to follow this up with some expression of our gladness at your return. A sum of £630 was raised for this. A recent referendum has disclosed the fact that the great majority would prefer to receive their gift in money. In order not to reduce the share which each would receive in the division of this sum the Committee are not spending any of it on a reception or entertainment but are sending it to you by post.

    We are conscious that no gift can be any sort of compensation for what the war has demanded of you but with the enclosed cheque we offer you our warm congratulations on your safe return and our best wishes for a happy future.

        We are,
           Yours faithfully,

                H. Cawley, Chairman, Victory Committee.
                Arthur Gage, Hon. Secretary.
                E. M. Cuming, Hon. Treasurer.

The joys of welcoming home those who had served was not confined to families and close friends. Whole communities joined in and 'Welcome Home Committees' were formed to arrange official tributes, as here at Uplyme. All Uplyme's servicemen and women received a five-pound note in an envelope like the one above.

In common with many other streets in Sidmouth, Brewery Lane staged a VE Day party for its children at which one of the many treats was ice cream sent by the American forces at Dunkeswell. Over fifty children tucked in and each later received sixpence. A *Sidmouth Herald* report of the time tells that 'they made their way to 'Nappy Peaseland' where races took place, including a race for mothers and fathers. Later, a recently returned POW from Germany lit a huge bonfire at the top of the road and an effigy of Hitler and a Swastika flag were burnt.' Parents kept the party going until midnight.

Exeter Old Contemptibles at a reunion in around 1952. They were so named after the Kaiser referred to the British Expeditionary Force of 1914 as 'a contemptible little army'.

In an age when Britain's overseas aid budget is considerable, it is perhaps sobering to recall that rationing continued long enough after World War Two for developing members of the Commonwealth to send *us* food parcels. Here Honiton's Deputy Mayor, Alderman Fred Studley, distributes Gift Food from the Tanganyika Food for Britain Fund at Dar-es-Salaam at the St Margaret's Alms Houses, Exeter Road, Honiton, in April 1949. Receiving the first gift is Mr Vanstone. The gift consisted of a tin of casserole steak and a tin of beef dripping. The dripping was part of a consignment of 100 cases.

128 Wessex Field Ambulance Territorials during manoeuvres on Woodbury Common, *c.* 1960.

Cyprus became a British Crown Colony in 1925 after first being ceded by the Turks to the British in 1878 and then annexed at the outbreak of World War One. It was an important Middle East base during World War Two and the immediate post-war period. Archbishop Makarios, advocating union with Greece, led a struggle for independence (1954-60) which resulted in Cyprus's becoming a republic in the British Commonwealth in 1961. Fighting between the Greek and Turkish communities in 1963 resulted in a UN force being sent. It was around that time that Honiton GP, Dr Terry Glanville, went to the island as Forces Medical officer. He is seen here checking the quality of the grape harvest at BMH Dekalia.

The June 1990 issue of the *Swedebasher* commemorates the fiftieth anniversary of the formation of the 12th Devons. Dick Sweetland, who edited the *Swedebasher* from its early days in Normandy (see p. 110) and for a further forty-two years, was awarded the British Empire Medal for his work in 1987. Below, Dick is pictured (extreme right) at the ceremony in Exeter at which he received the medal from the Lord Lieutenant of Devon, the Earl of Morley (centre).

12th (Airborne) Devons Branch of the Regimental Association

President: Major W. F. BARROW, M.B.E.

Vice-President: Colonel E. J. WARREN, D.S.O.

Secretary/Treasurer:
Richard G. SWEETLAND, B.E.M.

58 ALEXANDRIA ROAD, SIDMOUTH, DEVON, EX10 9HG – Tel (0395) 516697

1940   S W E D E B A S H E R   1945

Born in Battle .... To Live in Peace

No.147. Anniversary year of Airborne Forces and 12th Devons. JUNE, 1990.
Fifty – and still Bashing on Regardless !

Happy Half Century, Paras, Glider Boys and 12th Battalion, Beach Defence (1940-43) and Airborne (1943-45), The Devonshire Regiment. We've come a long way since those beach defences along the East Devon coastline.... and all that sickbag drill during those training flights that made us so airworthy !

But sadness for us all in April when GEORGE LEWIS, most popular C.S.M., and later R.S.M., died suddenly at Guildford, Surrey, on 20th April. He will always be remembered as the Gentleman R.S.M. Funeral Service was held at Guildford Crematorium on 26th April. Three Swedebashers who so kindly attended took along a 12th Devons floral tribute.

Our thoughts are with George's Widow, Marie, and Family. A True Swedebasher, George did much to create the Friendships we all enjoy today.

Our Chairman, Captain W.F.Robinson, told us that Mrs.Dorothy Bowman, Widow of our former Mortars Officer and Adjutant, David Bowman,M.C., died in Australia last year. We send our sympathies to Joy, their Daughter.

Since space is limited the following information and news is contracted into as small a space as that rum ration we got so little of when the weather was awful in Normandy ! REG WARRICK (London FW6) assures us that BRITTANY FERRIES on their PORTSMOUTH to CAEN (Ouistreham) voyages offer a 15% discount for all Airborne people (including next-of-kin, we think) but you've got to "stick up for your rights" to obtain this....

You'll read in this issue of FRANK and DOREEN PAYNE (Otterton, near Budleigh Salterton) celebrating their 50th Wedding Anniversary. They, and Grandson, Steve, came through loud and clear on our local BBC Devon Radio. Steve got a Rolls-Royce for the happy couple to go to a Honiton church on the day and two Swedebashers and Wives, Dick and Ann Wraxall (Axminster) and your Scribe and Wife helped "push the boat out" the night after !

John Eden (Carnforth, Lancs) and his Wife, were thrilled with their tour of the Rhine Crossing area in March. His report was most detailed and we hope to publish in No.148...... DAVID G.FLETCHER, 4,GLEN COTTAGES, JEWLSPON ROAD, UNDLOCK, POLEGATE, Sussex,BN26 3RX (tel. 03212 2483) of our Recce Platoon is a "lost sheep returned to the fold"...Thank-you, MAJOR GENERAL COLIN SHORTIS, Colonel of The Regiment, for your outstanding leadership during your term of office, especially for the "uplift" you've given to this Journal and its Editor. As we write Sidmouth remains the SWEDEBASHER HQ. We're as static as a grounded glider but hope to "take off" when the flight conditions improve !! We still Bash on Regardless !!!

ROYAL ARMY SERVICE CORPS · ALDERSHOT.

Emrys 'Sam' Pearce of Chardstock joined the
Royal Army Service Corp for National Service in
1947. He is pictured below with the vehicle
recovery unit he served with in Kenya. He left for
the UK and demobilization shortly before the
Mau Mau troubles began.

On 25 June 1950 the North Koreans invaded South Korea and rapidly drove the UN forces under General McArthur back into a small pocket around Pusan. Counter-attacking, the UN fought their way back, reaching the 38th parallel and then the Manchurian border. Alarmed, China sent 250,000 troops to aid the North Koreans and the UN forces were pushed back again. Eventually, with the two armies facing each other more-or-less along the 38th parallel, an armistice was signed in 1953. Total UN casualties were 118,515 killed and 264,238 wounded. British troops among those who served included 32 Medium Regiment Royal Artillery, seen here just after the ceasefire was signed, under canvas and on manoeuvres on the 38th parallel. Gunner Don Rodgers, from Seaton but now living at Axminster, is on the left and can be seen again (below) near ammunition cases with a signals truck in the background.

Dudley Hurford of Kilmington served with the Devonshire Regiment in Kenya during his National Service and was wounded during action against the Mau Mau, the secret society drawn mainly from the Kikuyu tribe whose aim, during their terrorist campaign (1952-59), was to drive European settlers out of Kenya. Dudley is seen under canvas in the Aberdare mountains in 1953.

Keeping the Home Fires Burning. Task Force families have their minds taken off the Falkland War by a concert at ITC Royal Marines Lympstone.

Two views on modern war. Not everyone supported the Gulf War: seen in the centre, above, among people holding a peace vigil outside Exmouth's Magnolia Centre in January 1991, are the Grandmother(s) Against The Gulf War'. Below, gifts pour in for troops in the Falkland Islands in 1982. Left to right are Victor Burge, the collection organiser, John Hannam, Exeter's MP, and Cyril Owen, who made these Marsh Barton premises available to store the gifts.

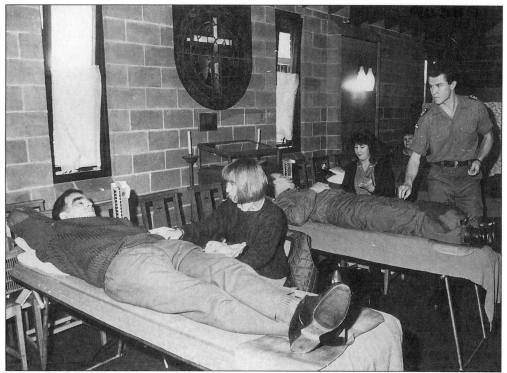

Not every Royal Marine could be sent to the Falkland Islands, of course. Those that stayed behind helped in other ways, including, here at the Commando Training Centre, Lympstone, giving blood.

'Welcome Home.' Kerry Mason, who served on HMS *Brilliant*, is greeted at Branscombe Close, Exeter, by his family on his return from the Falkland Islands in July 1982.

Seaton man Derek Anning (right) emigrated to Australia in the 1960s and joined the Australian Army in 1968, serving in all for six years. He spent a year on active service in Vietnam, where he was awarded the Vietnam Medal and the Vietnamese Campaign Medal, both of which he is wearing (right). Below Derek receives his medals from a Vietnamese general. Derek returned to England and now lives in Sidmouth.

Iain Sutherland of Colyton served in the Gulf War and is seen here taking a break from shifting sand with his Challenger tank in Kuwait in 1990. His parents, Graham and Cherry, on the left, found arranging the family celebrations for his homecoming (below) easy – they run the Kingfisher pub in the village.

The British Legion, later Royal British Legion, has fought for over seventy years for ex-servicemen and their dependents. Millions of pounds have been raised in ways ranging from the annual Poppy Day collections down to the humble whist drive and fête. At a Seaton branch British Legion fête in the Cricket Field on 15 July 1948, Vera Parsons ('The New Look') and Janet Gardner ('Mary, Mary, Quite Contrary') were among the prize winners.

Fifty Years On. The Royal British Legion standards are carried along Exmouth's sea front at the head of the parade in August 1995 that marked the fiftieth anniversary of VJ Day.

A CERTAIN CURE FOR THE

GERMAN MEASLES.

Mix some Woolwich Powders with Tinct. of Iron or Essence of Lead, and administer in pills (or shells). Have ready a little British Army (a little goes a long way) some Brussels Sprouts and French Mustered. Add a little Canadian Cheese and Australian Lamb and season with the best Indian Curry. Set it on a Kitchener and keep stirring until quite hot.

If this does not make the Patient perspire freely, rub the best Russian Bears' Grease on his chest and wrap in Berlin Wool.

Dr. Cannon's Prescrip.

P.S. -The patient must on no account have any Peace-Soup until the swelling in the head has quite disappeared.

Acknowledgements

We are especially grateful to Chris Wright, librarian at the *Express & Echo*, and to that paper's editor, Rachael Campey, for permission to research and make use of its extensive collection of old pictures of Exeter and district. Also to the Chief Constable, Mr John Evans, for permission to use items from the Force (Devon & Cornwall Constabulary) Museum and to the curator, Brian Estill, for his help and for an interesting and personal tour of the many exhibits in the museum. Also to the Axminster Museum and the Allhallows Museum at Honiton; to Donald S. King for permission to use his notes on the Axminster Volunteers and the East Devon Legion; and to Branscombe Parish Council, especially Elsie Mayo (archivist) and Linda Hughes (parish clerk). Branscombe's recording of its pictorial (and picturesque) past is a lesson to us all.

Others to allow us to use their photographs are Derek Anning, Douglas Arkle, Edith Bagwell, Jean Board, Noel Collier, Thelma Collier, Mike Davis, Bob and Ivy Ferguson, Thelma and the late Bill Finnemore, John Frost, Kathleen Gage, Mr and Mrs Albert Gardner, Terry Glanville, John Godfrey of the Seaton Book Centre, Stan and Stephanie Gudge, Peter Harris, Percy Heard, Pru Wakley, Frank Huddy, Dudley Hurford, Jean Luxton and Exeter Wheelers, William Manley, Syd Middleton, Les Mitchell, Emrys 'Sam' Pearce, Jim Perriam, Mary Priddle, Gladys Pile, Glyn Roberts, Don Rodgers, James Rowe, Margorie Rowe, Cecil and Kath Sansom, Les Sloman, Joy Seward, Barbara and Alan Softly, Sidbury's honorary archivists, Bill Snell, Elsie Stennett, Gwen Studley, Alice 'Jin' Sweetland, Bob Tall, Vera Tanner, Henry Trenchard, Frank Webber, Ivy and Alan Young. Our thanks to them all.

In a different direction we thank the staff at Chalford Publishing Company, especially Simon Thraves, for putting up with us.